Prayers
That Avail Much
for Kids

Prayers That Avail Much for Kids

Short and Simple Prayers
Packed With the Power of God's Word

by
Germaine Copeland
Word Ministries, Inc.

Harrison House

Scripture quotations are taken from the *International Children's Bible,*
New Century Version (ICB), copyright © 1986, 1988 by Word Publishing, Dallas, Texas 75039.

Scripture quotations marked (NKJV) are taken from *The New King James Version.*
Copyright © 1979, 1980, 1982. Thomas Nelson, Inc. Used by permission. All rights reserved

Scriptures marked (KJV) are taken from the *King James Version* of the Bible.

Illustrations are by Elizabeth Linder.

Prayers That Avail Much For Kids —
Short and Simple Prayers Packed With the Power of God's Word
ISBN 0-89274-956-3
Copyright © 1996 by Germaine Copeland
Word Ministries, Inc.
38 Sloan Street
Roswell, Georgia 30075

4th Printing

Published by Harrison House, Inc.
P. O. Box 35035
Tulsa, Oklahoma 74153

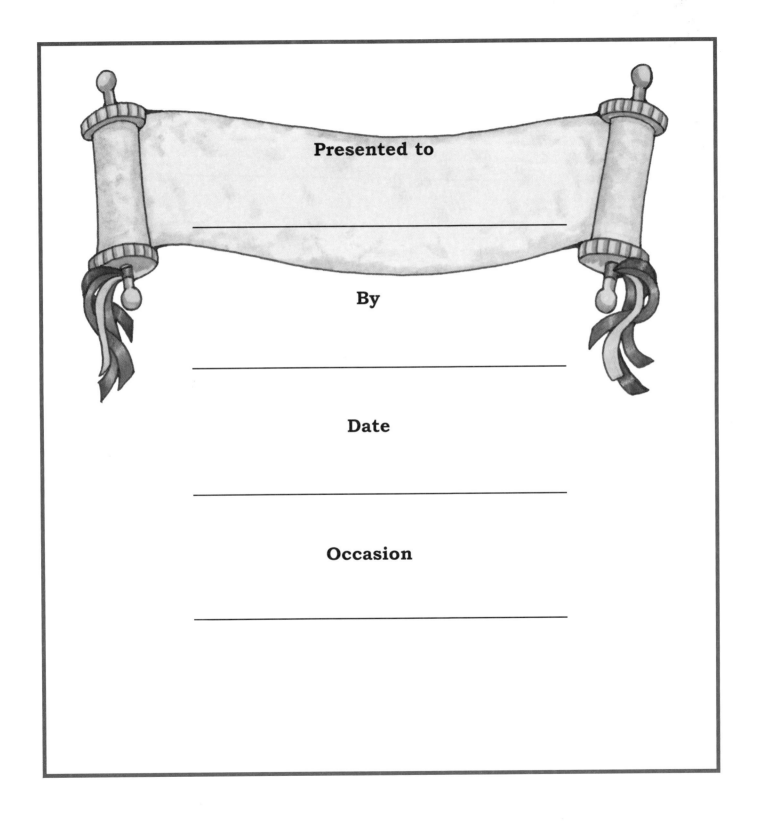

Presented to

By

Date

Occasion

Contents

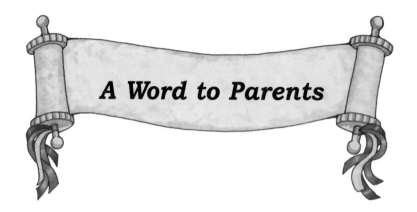

A Word to Parents

This book was written to help you, a parent, begin instilling in your children at an early age the knowledge that God loves them so much He sent Jesus to destroy the works of the devil so that anyone who believes in Jesus can live an abundant, victorious life.

Read the book aloud to your children or encourage them to read it to themselves aloud. As they hear the Scriptures, faith will begin to build in their hearts because "...faith cometh by hearing, and hearing by the word of God" (Romans 10:17 KJV). As they hear or read the Scriptures, prayers and confessions again and again, their minds will become renewed to God's Word. Encourage your children to meditate on the Scriptures by thinking about how they can apply the principles and prayers to specific situations in their lives and in the lives of those around them.

By spending time reading and meditating the Scriptures, applying the prayers to actual situations and speaking the confessions over themselves, your children will learn through practical application how to spend time building their relationship with God and the importance of giving

Him and His Word first place in their lives. Your children will begin to speak the Word with the power and authority available to them through Jesus. They will learn to walk in victory!

The prayer for praising God is the last one that appears in this book so that your children can turn to it easily. Encourage them to say this prayer often to help them understand the importance of praising and thanking God for Who He is and for what He has done as an important part of their relationship with Him.

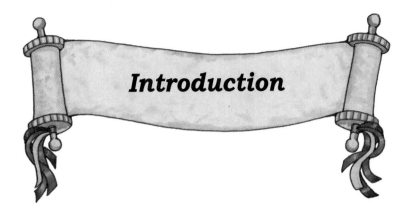

Introduction

God is good and wants good things for you. God loves you so much that He sent Jesus to earth to die, be buried, then come back to life through His Resurrection so that you can spend eternity with Him. When you say with your mouth and believe in your heart that God raised Jesus from the dead, you will be saved and be with Him always. (Romans 10:9, 10.)

Read the Scriptures in this book aloud or listen carefully as someone reads them to you. Pray the prayers over specific things that happen in your life and in other people's lives. The Bible tells us in James 5:16, "When a good man prays, great things happen." A "good man" is someone (a man or woman, boy or girl) who is made good by God when they believe in Jesus.

Pray and ask God to do the things He promises us in the Bible and great things will happen!

When God answers your prayers, thank Him and tell others what He has done for you. Tell them how to receive Jesus into their hearts so that Jesus can be their friend and they can know this awesome God, too!

"Thanks be to God, who always leads us in victory through Christ!"

(2 Corinthians 2:14).

> *If you use your mouth to say, "Jesus is Lord," and if you believe in your heart that God raised Jesus from death, then you will be saved. We believe with our hearts, and so we are made right with God. And we use our mouths to say that we believe, and so we are saved.*
> Romans 10:9, 10

Father God,

Thank You for raising Jesus from the dead after He died on the cross and defeated the devil for me. I believe in my heart that Jesus paid for my sins on the cross. I am so happy to say, "Come into my heart, Lord Jesus. I am born again into God's family." In Jesus' Name, amen.

Say this:

Jesus is always with me.

Made New

We love because God first loved us.
1 John 4:19

...nothing...will ever be able to separate us from the
love of God that is in Christ Jesus our Lord.
Romans 8:38, 39

Father God,

Thank You that You sent Jesus as my Savior and that You love me even when I make a mistake. Thank You so much for Your love for me. In Jesus' Name, amen.

Say this:
God loves me. Jesus loves me.

God Loves Me

> *"Love the Lord your God. Love him with all your heart, all your soul, all your mind, and all your strength."*
>
> *The second most important command is this: "Love your neighbor as you love yourself." These two commands are the most important commands.*
> *Mark 12:30, 31*

Father God:

Help me to love myself then to love others the same way. In Jesus' Name, amen.

Say this:

I love my neighbors as I love myself.

Loving Others

Jesus answered, "I am the way. And I am the truth and the life. The only way to the Father is through me. If you really knew me, then you would know my Father, too...."
John 14:6, 7

Father God,

Thank You for sending Your Son, Jesus, to be the way to You and to show me what You are like. Help me understand Who You are and how much You love Me. In Jesus' Name, amen.

Say this:
**As I learn more about Jesus,
I will know God better.**

Knowing God

"For God loved the world so much that he gave his only Son. God gave his Son so that whoever believes in him may not be lost, but have eternal life."
John 3:16

Father God,
    Teach me how to show Your love to my friends and tell them about Jesus. In Jesus' Name, amen.

Say this:
God will help me tell my friends about Jesus so that they can live forever with Him.

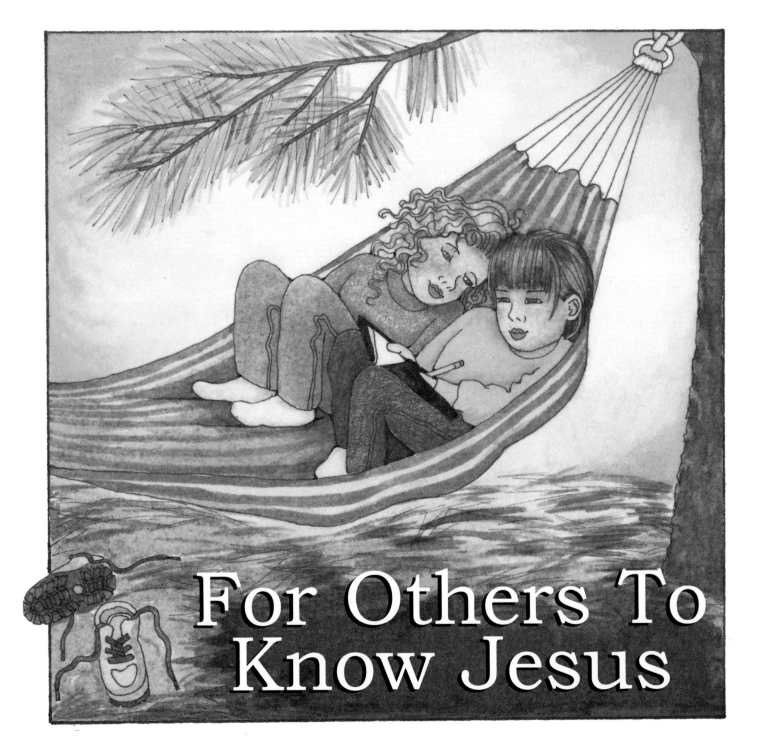

For Others To
Know Jesus

21

It takes wisdom to have a good family. It takes understanding to make it strong. It takes knowledge to fill a home with rare and beautiful treasures.
Proverbs 24:3, 4

Father God:

Help me to use my words and my actions to build up my family instead of to tear them down. In Jesus' Name, amen.

Say this:
God shows me how to understand my family. He shows me what to say and do to help them and be kind to them.

My Family

...“It is more blessed to give than to receive.”
Acts 20:35

Father God,

Help me to share the things I have with others who maybe don't have those things. Thank You that because I share I am blessed. In Jesus' Name, amen.

Say this:
I help others by sharing my things with them.

Helping
Others

I go to bed and sleep in peace. Lord, only you keep me safe.
Psalm 4:8

Father God,

I thank You that as I go to sleep, I have no fear. You keep me safe. In Jesus' Name, amen.

Say this:
The Lord keeps me safe as I sleep.

Peaceful Sleep

...if you trust in the Lord, you will be safe.
Proverbs 29:25

Father God,

Thank You that because I trust You, I will be safe today. You will keep me from harm. In Jesus' Name, amen.

Say this:
I trust the Lord and He keeps me safe.

Safety and Protection

You must worship the Lord your God. If you do,
I [God] will bless your bread and your water.
I will take away sickness from you.
Exodus 23:25

Father God,

   Thank You for providing food for me to eat. Thank You that You provide for my needs and that You take sickness away from me. In Jesus' Name, amen.

Say this:
The Lord blesses my food and takes sickness away from me.

My Food

Christ carried our sins in his body on the cross. He did this so that we would stop living for sin and start living for what is right. And we are healed because of his wounds.
1Peter 2:24

Father God,

I believe in my heart that Jesus took sickness away from me. I receive healing for my body, in Jesus' Name, amen.

Say this:
By Jesus' wounds I am healed.

Free From Being Sick

But the Holy Spirit will come to you. Then you will receive power. You will be my witnesses — in Jerusalem, in all of Judea, in Samaria, and in every part of the world.
Acts 1:8

Father God,

You gave Your disciples power to tell others about Jesus. You have promised me this power also. I receive Your Holy Spirit right now, in Jesus' Name, amen.

Say this:
Thank You, Father God, for filling me with Your Holy Spirit.

Holy Spirit
In Me

In all your ways acknowledge Him, and He shall direct your paths.
Proverbs 3:6 NKJV

Father God,

Please help me find my _____.
I ask the Holy Spirit to show me where to look. In Jesus' Name, amen.

Say this:
Thank You for helping me find my _____.

Looking for Something Lost

Children, obey your parents in all things.
This pleases the Lord.
Colossians 3:20

Father God,

Help me to obey my parents and the grown-ups they have trusted to watch over me today. It pleases You when I obey them. In Jesus' Name, amen.

Say this:
I do what my parents ask me to do because this pleases the Lord.

Obeying My Parents

Happy is the nation whose God is the Lord.
Happy are the people He chose for his very own.
Psalm 33:12

Father God,

Thank You for my country.
Help the people in my country to
know Jesus as their Savior and to
serve You. In Jesus' Name, amen.

Say this:
**Because the people in my
country serve Jesus, we are
happy.**

My Nation

Jesus said to the followers, "Go everywhere in the world. Tell the Good News to everyone."
Mark 16:15

Father God,

   Thank You that You told me I could go to other places and tell people about Jesus. I want to tell people the Good News that You love them. Bless the people who have gone to other places to share the Good News. In Jesus' Name, amen.

Say this:

I will tell people the Good News about Jesus wherever I go.

Missionaries

I will praise the Lord all my life. I will sing praises to my God as long as I live.
Psalm 146:2

Father God,

I praise You for Your greatness. I praise You because You love me. I thank You for all the good things You have done for me and given me. In Jesus' Name, amen.

Say this:
I will praise God all my life.

Praising God

Other Books by Word Ministries, Inc.

Prayers That Avail Much — Volume 1

Prayers That Avail Much — Volume 1
portable gift book

Prayers That Avail Much — Volume 2

Prayers That Avail Much — Volume 2
portable gift book

Prayers That Avail Much — Volume 3

Oraciones Con Poder

Prayers That Avail Much
Spanish Edition

Prayers That Avail Much for Business Professionals

Prayers That Avail Much — Special Edition

Prayers That Avail Much for Mothers
pocket size

Prayers That Avail Much for Mothers
leather

Prayers That Avail Much for Fathers

Prayers That Avail Much for Teens
revised pocket edition

Prayers That Avail Much Daily Calendar

Available From Your Local Bookstore

Harrison House

Word Ministries, Inc.
38 Sloan Street * Roswell, Georgia 30075

The Harrison House Vision
Proclaiming the truth and the power
Of the Gospel of Jesus Christ
With Excellence;
Challenging Christians to
Live victoriously,
Grow Spiritually,
Know God intimately.